COLOR WITH
STICKERS
SPACE

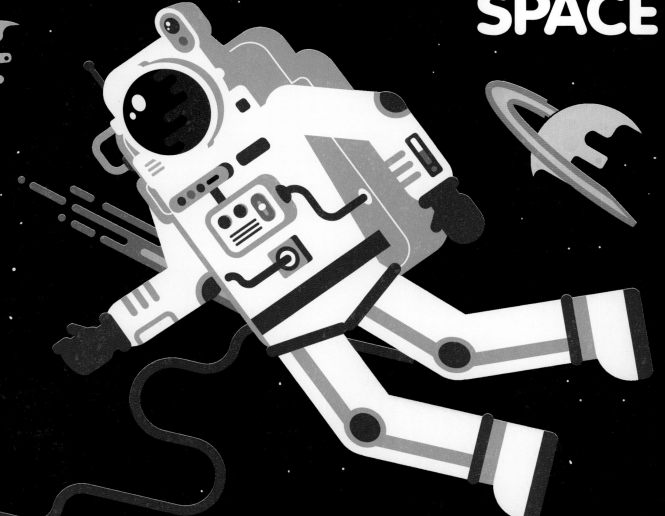

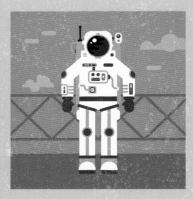

tiger 🐯 tales

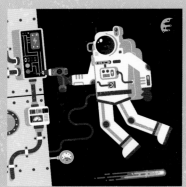

tiger tales

5 River Road, Suite 128, Wilton, CT 06897
Published in the United States 2021
Originally published in Great Britain 2021
by Caterpillar Books Ltd.
Text by Jonny Marx
Text copyright © 2021 Caterpillar Books Ltd.
Illustrations copyright © SHUTTERSTOCK.COM
ISBN-13: 978-1-6643-4010-7
ISBN-10: 1-6643-4010-6
Printed in China
CPB/3800/1673/1020
2 4 6 8 10 9 7 5 3 1

www.tigertalesbooks.com

Welcome to a wonderful world of stickers!

Are you ready to make some awesome rockets, space stations, and solar systems?

Match each numbered sticker on the sticker sheet in the back of the book to the same number on the picture.

You can even customize your creations with some of the extra stickers on the sticker sheet.

Look at the back of each page to learn fun facts about the scenes you make!

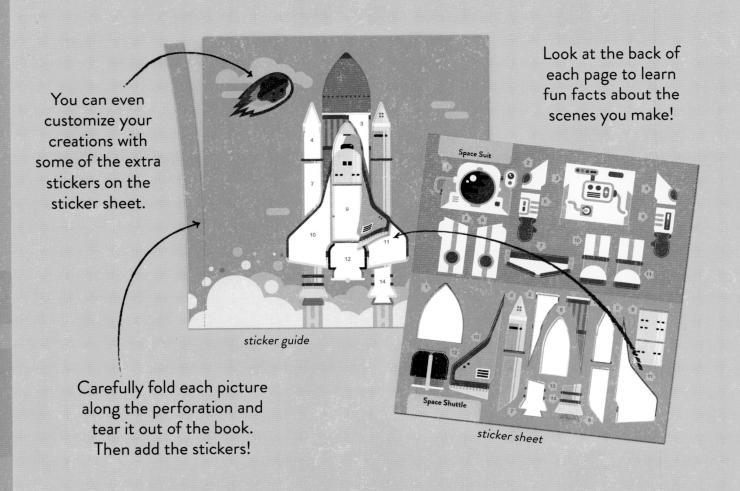

sticker guide

sticker sheet

Carefully fold each picture along the perforation and tear it out of the book. Then add the stickers!

WHAT IS SPACE?

Most of the universe is space — enormous, empty space!

Planets, stars, asteroids, comets, moons, and more
take up only a tiny amount of this huge area.

When you look up at the sky on a clear night,
you can see "twinkling" stars. These are actually suns in other
solar systems that are so far away, they look like small dots.

We live on planet Earth, and we know a lot about it.
But there are millions and millions of planets in space,
and millions of galaxies. There's so much more to explore!

Space Suit

If you were to travel into space without a
spacecraft or suit, you would blow up like a balloon!

Astronauts wear space suits for protection.

The space suit gives astronauts the air they need to breathe.
It also helps them stay warm or keep cool. In space, it
can be colder than a freezer and warmer than an oven!

A space suit can cost as much as $12 million.

Space suits are made of special
rip-proof materials.

Space Shuttle

Unlike rockets, space shuttles can't travel far
into space. Instead, they travel a short distance to
help carry materials and supplies to space stations.

The fuel needed to launch a space shuttle
could fill a swimming pool.

A space shuttle can travel more than
six times quicker than a speeding bullet!

The shuttle can take flight from a launch pad,
but it can also take off and land
just like an airplane.

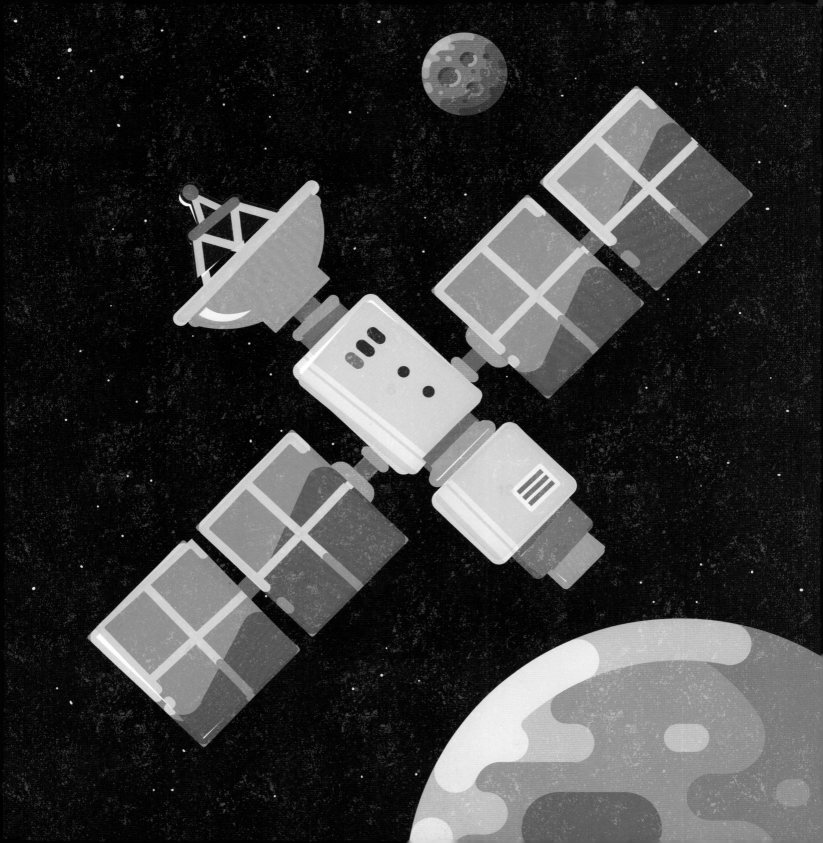

Satellite

A satellite is any (human-made) object
that circles around a planet or moon.

There are thousands of satellites traveling around Earth.
Some of these are used to help us make our telephone
calls, or to plan our journeys when we drive!
Others look at the weather and how our
planet is changing. Some look into
outer space to help us explore.

We've even launched satellites
toward other planets!

Solar System

There are eight planets, more than two
hundred moons, thousands of asteroids,
and one sun in our solar system.

The Sun is a big burning ball of gas. It produces light and heat.

Mercury is the smallest planet in our solar system.

Venus is the hottest planet.

Earth is one-third land and two-thirds water.

Mars is known as the red planet because it is covered in rusty dust.

Saturn has huge rings made of ice and rock.

Uranus is the coldest planet in our solar system.

Neptune has winds that can travel faster than jet planes.

There are millions and millions of solar systems
in the universe, each with a sun
at its center.

Rover

Rovers are like cars, but they run
on battery power. They can travel over
dusty, uneven ground, just like the terrain
you'd find on the surface of the Moon, or Mars.

Some rovers are remote-controlled.

Scientists have sent several rovers to the Moon
and to explore the surface of Mars; the
first reached the planet in 1997.

In 2018, a dust storm on Mars destroyed
a rover called Opportunity.

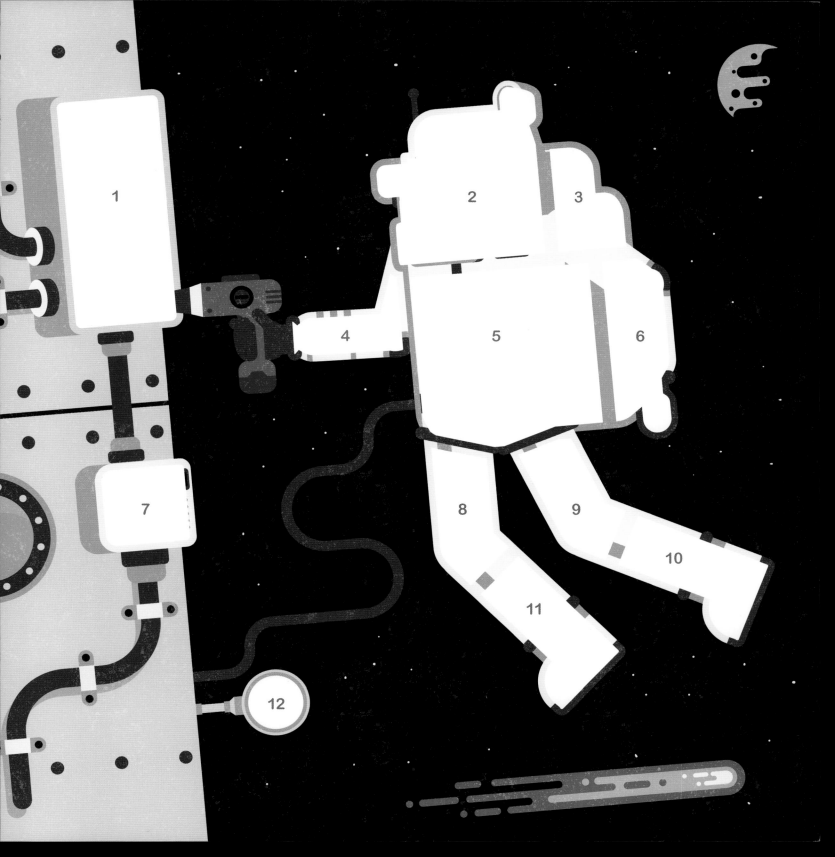

Spacewalking

Astronauts perform spacewalks when they travel outside a spacecraft. Each astronaut has to be connected to the craft with a tether so that they don't drift into space.

Astronauts can make repairs to their ships when spacewalking.

Some astronauts wear jet packs when they spacewalk. These packs send out small jets of air to push the astronaut in different directions.

Lunar Lander

Landers are used to transport astronauts and equipment to the surface of a planet or moon.

The Apollo lunar lander was used in 1969. It transported Neil Armstrong and Buzz Aldrin from their spacecraft to the surface of the Moon (and then back again). They became the first astronauts to walk on the Moon.

Landers have now been designed to explore Mars.

Space Station

A space station is like a hotel, although it's cramped, and the guests float in midair! Astronauts live on space stations while completing missions.

The International Space Station (ISS) can travel around Earth in just 90 minutes!

Flowers and food, including lettuce, radishes, and peas, have been grown on the ISS.

The ISS is as big as a football field!

Six astronauts live on the ISS at any given time.

When they're not working, the astronauts can watch TV!

Rockets

Rockets come in all shapes and sizes.
Some are used to send satellites into space,
others to transport astronauts and supplies,
and some to explore and complete experiments.

Scientists are now making rockets to
help transport tourists at thrilling speed!
You may even be able to visit space without
being an astronaut, but a ticket to
board each flight is likely to
be very expensive!

Space Exploration

Space is absolutely enormous! So big, in fact, that we haven't been able to explore much of what it has to offer.

We've been to the Moon, and we've used big lenses, called telescopes, to look at distant galaxies and stars, but we still have not visited our closest neighbor, Mars.

Scientists are almost certain, however, that we'll travel to Mars within the next 30 years.

Maybe you'll be the first astronaut to visit!

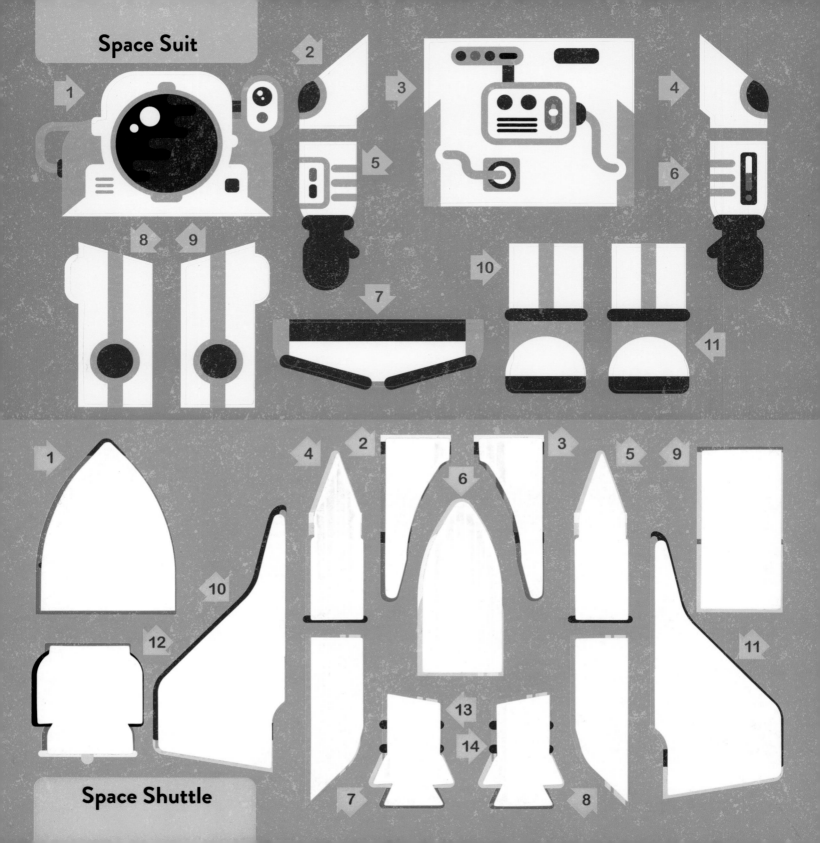

Space Suit

Space Shuttle

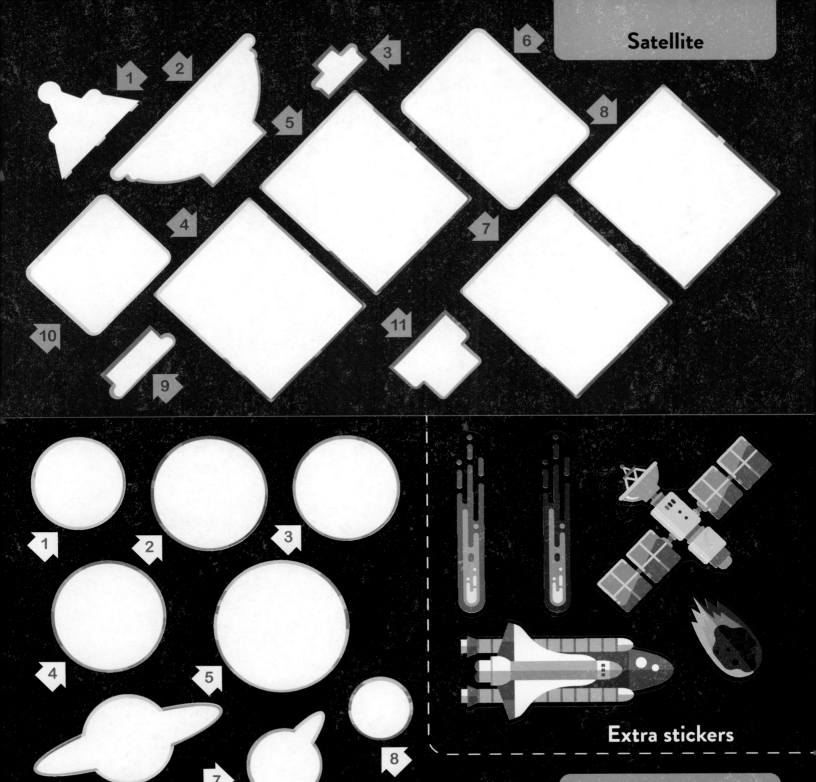

Satellite

Extra stickers

Solar Sytem

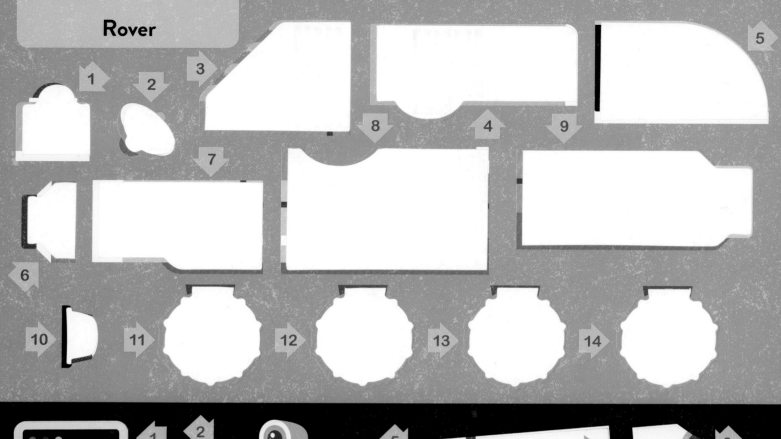

Rover

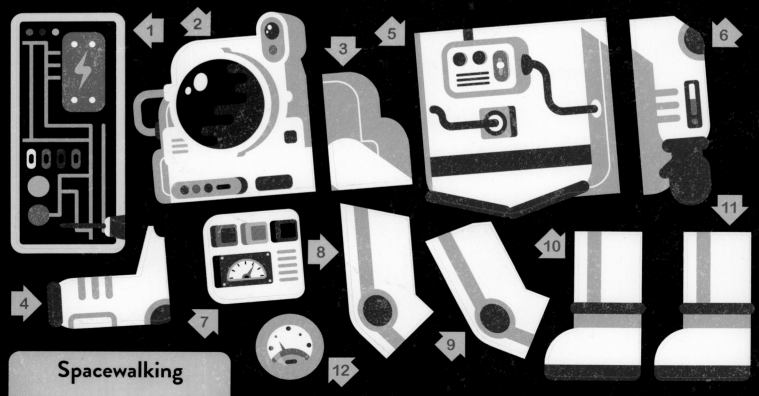

Spacewalking

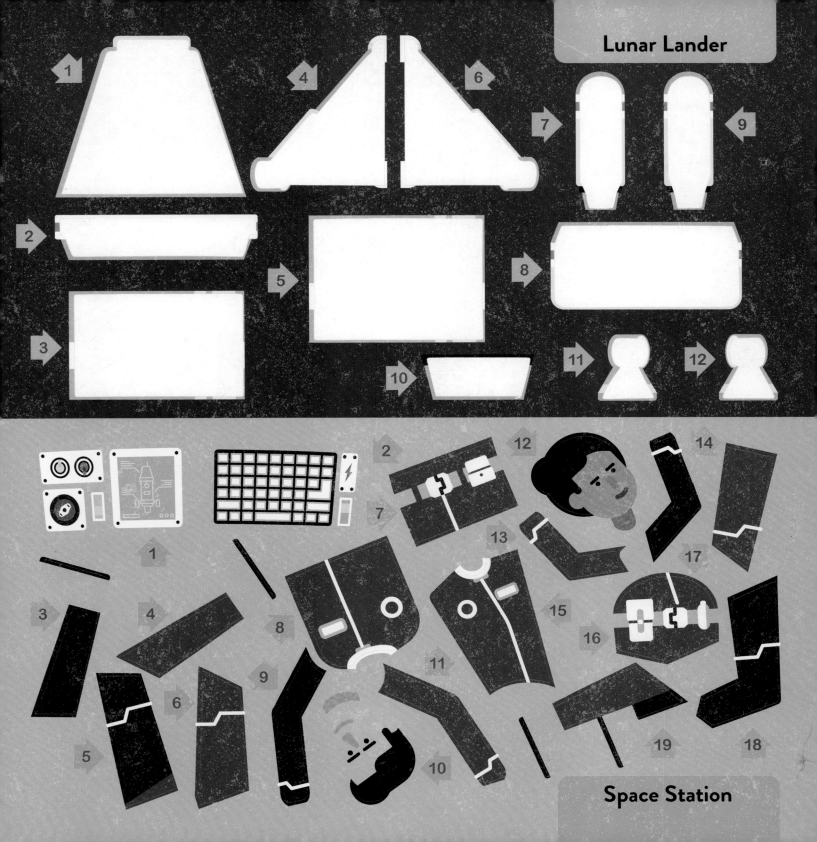

Lunar Lander

Space Station

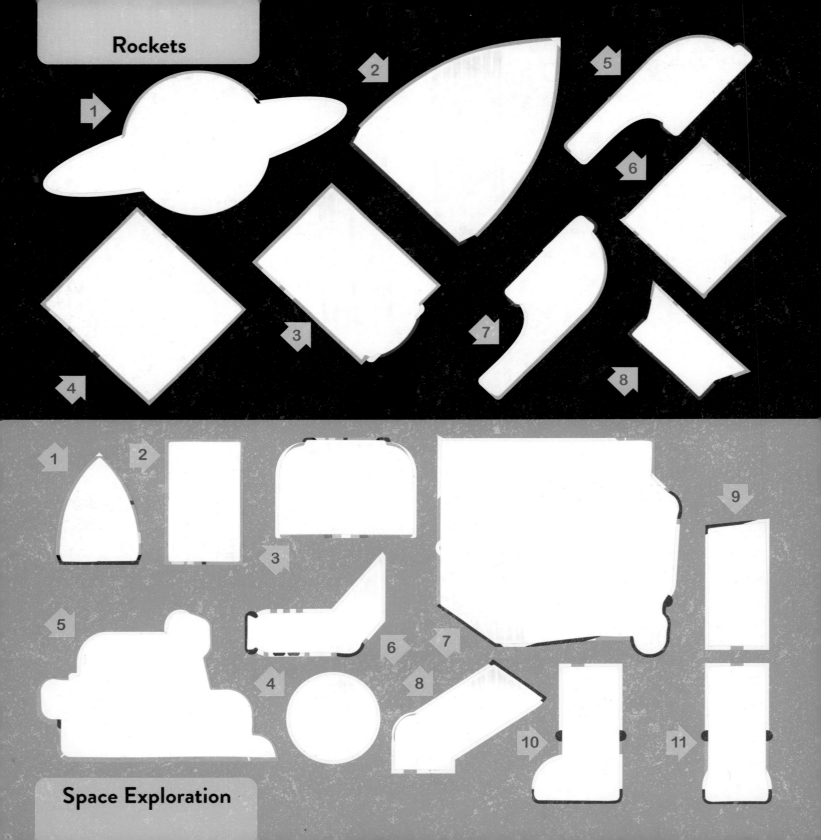

Rockets

Space Exploration